Two Lectures on the Gospels

Two Papers on the Parish

Two Lectures on the Gospels

by F. Crawford Burkitt, M.A.
Trinity College, Cambridge

WIPF & STOCK · Eugene, Oregon

Wipf and Stock Publishers
199 W 8th Ave, Suite 3
Eugene, OR 97401

Two Lectures on the Gospels
By Burkitt, F. Crawford
ISBN 13: 978-1-5326-1277-0
Publication date 10/20/2016
Previously published by Macmillan & Co., Limited, 1901

CONTENTS

The two Lectures here printed were delivered at the University Extension Summer Meeting, Cambridge, 1900.

TWO LECTURES ON THE GOSPELS

THE nineteenth century has been an eventful period in the study of the Bible as well as in other departments of learning. Ancient documents of great importance have been discovered, and many very fruitful investigations have been made upon special points, by the aid of which we are enabled to attack with larger resources and a better hope of success the great problems that still remain unsolved. But the condition of New Testament study is in one point very different from that of Old Testament study. There is no dominant theory before us like that of Graf and Wellhausen, who, by putting the Prophets before the Law, have enabled us for the first time to see the history of Israel in its true perspective. The older

traditions about the origins of the New Testament are much more trustworthy than those
about the Old, and the greatest advance has
been not so much in new dates for the documents as in the way that the investigators have
come to look at them.   In a word, the position
gained has been the general adoption of the
historical point of view.

From the historical point of view the scholar
aims at seeing things as they were, taking
account of the struggles and even the prejudices
of the time under consideration, while seeking
as far as possible to forget the controversies
and prejudices of his own day.   The business
of the historian is to trace the course of past
events ; to explain, rather than to judge.   Put
in the abstract it sounds rational enough, but
as a matter of fact the conditions under which
this ideal could be even faintly realised in the
case of New Testament study have never been
present before our own days.

In the Middle Ages the dominant theory of
the Christian Church had no rivals.   Men did
not know of and could hardly conceive a state
of things in which the machinery of Catholicism
did not exist.   There could be but little Biblical

criticism, little independent study of the Bible, because the Bible was authenticated by the unchallenged authority of the Church, and it was believed to exist for the purpose of proving the Church's doctrine. With the Reformation came a new era. One of the chief weapons of all parties of the Reformers had been the patent discrepancy between the Church as then governed and the Church as pourtrayed in the New Testament. For a moment, as it were, the Bible had been looked at with an open eye. But the results of that hasty glance were so far-reaching that Protestants turned away from further unprejudiced study to make good the position they had already won. The Reformers of the sixteenth century broke with the Roman polity and refashioned their church to what they considered to be the Apostolic model. Some, like Calvin and Knox, built it up afresh from the ground ; others, like the English Reformers, were content with what our architects are fond of calling a *thorough conservative restoration*. But when the age of reconstruction was passed, the energies of Protestant scholars were set to a task not essentially different from those

of their Catholic brethren : they were more
occupied in proving the doctrines of their own
communion out of the New Testament than in
setting themselves to investigate the true
characteristics and development of the early
Church.

In the eighteenth century matters were
even less favourable to historical research. It
was an age of theory, an age of vigorous and
rigorous demonstration. Men wrote and
argued whether Christianity was " true " or
" false " : they did not ask " how did Christianity grow up ? " Of course we all believe
that the universe is governed by law and not
by caprice ; things really do come to pass with
the utmost vigour and rigour. But our ignor-
ance of some to us most interesting phases and
aspects of early Christianity is so profound
that ready-made theories of how things ought
to have happened are often falsified by the
event.

As I said at the beginning, the nineteenth
century has been an eventful period in New
Testament criticism ; in many ways it has
marked a new era. This is partly due to
discoveries of unknown or lost documents which

have thrown light upon points hitherto obscure,
but still more is due to that increased interest
in the study of Embryology, as applied to organ-
ised institutions as well as to single individuals
and races, which has followed the victory of
the idea of evolution.   The study of religions
has become a department of Natural History.
It is true that we do not pretend to explain
what Life really is ; but though we have for
the most part ceased to sit in judgment, we
are learning more accurately and more intelligently to describe.

  What, then, are the problems before us ?

  It was impossible adequately to touch upon
all the subjects connected with New Testament
study in the course of a couple of lectures, and
I find that I shall have to confine my remarks
to the Gospels.

  The study of the Gospels may be divided
here for convenience into two branches, which
may be called *Textual Criticism* and *Introduction*.   Under the head of " Introduction "
we may group all those questions which are
really concerned with the first appearance of a
book, such as the date, place of publication, the
authorship, and the sources known to or used

by the author. Under the head of " Textual Criticism " comes the history of the book from the time it left the author's hands to the present day, including the study not only of accidental errors introduced by copyists, but also of the work of later editors and revisers. A third branch, that of *Interpretation*, should be added, but it will hardly come in to the scope of these Lectures.

LECTURE I

" The fact, however, remains to be accounted for that very early in the history of the Church there came to be differences between the Gospels as read at Rome and at Alexandria."

SALMON, Some Thoughts, p. 144.

" I think that critics will not ultimately acquiesce in Hort's view that this conclusion [Mk. xvi 9–20] is a piece of an independent narrative which some one chose to append to St. Mark's Gospel, but will believe that it was from the first composed for the purpose for which it has served, at any rate since the time of Irenæus, to bring the second Gospel to a more satisfactory termination."

Ibid. p. 155.

THE TEXT OF THE FOUR GOSPELS

TEXTUAL Criticism is a subject which has, I
fear, to many people a rather dry and technical
sound.   I do not intend, however, to weary you
with a long discussion upon the various systems
of grouping the MSS., and of weighing their
merits, which are associated with the names of
Westcott and Hort, or of Burgon and Scrivener.
I would rather refer you to the little work of
Dr. Salmon called *Some Thoughts on the Textual
Criticism of the New Testament*, which I put
down in the list of works recommended for study
to those who attend these Lectures.   In that
lively and stimulating book you will find some
acute criticism of the weaker points in Dr. Hort's
Introduction, while at the same time it is re-
cognised that Dr. Hort's theory still holds the
field against its older antagonists.   Nor shall
I enter upon any of the newer textual theories.

The fact is that in no other department of New Testament study has the discovery of fresh documents so materially added to our knowledge and altered the balance of the evidence. We are still in the transition period between the new and the old, but it is beginning to be clear in what direction the next move is to be.

As you are no doubt aware, Dr. Hort regarded the majority of Greek MSS. of the New Testament as either the direct product of a revision of the text made early in the fourth century or to have been largely contaminated by that revision, while for the reconstruction of the true text he laid the utmost weight upon the MS. generally called B, a fourth century copy of the whole Greek Bible preserved in the Vatican Library. This theory was violently attacked at the time it appeared, nearly twenty years ago, by the late Dean Burgon, who defended the text of the mass of Greek MSS. and regarded the text of B as corrupt. But on one point both Dean Burgon and Dr. Hort were agreed in common with other textual critics : they held that the texts generally called " Western " were inferior and corrupted.

Now the remarkable point about this was

that the so-called "Western" texts have by far the best external claim to apostolic antiquity. Dr. Hort shows that you cannot trace back the type of text found in ordinary Greek MSS. beyond the end of the third century: Dean Burgon held, and subsequent investigation has confirmed the view, that the particular type of text found in B has some connexion with the great Alexandrian scholar Origen (✝ 250 A.D.) and cannot be traced back beyond him. But pieces of evidence dating from the second century, such as the quotations of Justin Martyr, the recension of St. Luke's Gospel put forward by the heretic Marcion, and even the quotations of the Alexandrian Clement, are all found to contain many "Western" readings; nevertheless "Western" texts as a whole found no favour with modern critics.

The reason of this was not far to seek. The support of Justin Martyr and other early writers showed that "Western" authorities attested some ancient readings not to be found elsewhere, but the best preserved and best edited "Western" texts were not the purest representatives of their class. The misleading name "Western" was originally given to these texts, because until half a century ago the MSS. known to scholars which contained them were either Greek MSS. written in the west of Europe or copies of the Old Latin versions. Without going into details we may fairly say that textual critics had formerly to choose between the text approved by an Alexandrian scholar in A.D. 250 and the texts current in Italy about A.D. 350 : is it any wonder that of the two alternatives they chose the former ?

The quotations of ancient writers supply evidence by which to test the quality of our MSS., but they do not supply their place ; what we want are documents which give us a continuous text untainted by critical revision and by the general mixture which followed Diocletian's persecution and the political triumph of Christianity. Such documents are very few. One of the best of them is Codex Bobiensis (*k*), containing the latter half of St. Mark and the first half of St. Matthew in Latin. This precious fragment preserves for us the text as read in Roman Africa about the time of St. Cyprian, *i.e.* in the middle of the third century. Where *k* is missing other Latin documents, notably Codex Palatinus (*e*), supply its place, but not with the same freedom from later admixture.[1]

Still more help now comes from the extreme East. From about the middle of the second century a Syriac-speaking Christian community had been established in the Euphrates valley, and before A.D. 200 it appears that the New Testament had been translated into their language. But the Syriac version of the New Testament known as the Peshitta is not this ancient translation, but a much later revision of it made to conform more closely to the Greek, just as the Latin Vulgate is a revision of the older Latin texts. A copy of the more ancient Syriac translation of the four Gospels was brought to England some fifty years ago, and its text published by Dr. Cureton in 1858. It was soon seen that this text contained many of the readings which had hitherto been regarded as exclusively characteristic of the MSS. of Western Europe.

But Cureton's MS. was very imperfect, not

[1] I may add that it was Dr. Hort himself who first drew attention to the excellence of *k* by pointing out the close resemblance of its text to the quotations of St. Cyprian. Yet even he occasionally hesitates to accept its evidence as decisive for North Africa, *e.g. Notes*, p. 45*a*.

more than half the contents of the Gospels
being preserved in it, and moreover (as we now
know) it does not give a very pure form of the
Old Syriac version, as it shows signs of having
been corrected in places by later Greek MSS.
The discovery of another MS. of the same
version in 1892 at the convent of St. Catherine
on Mount Sinai was therefore a great gain.
The new MS. was a palimpsest, and often very
hard to decipher, but not more than one-eighth
of the whole is actually lost or quite illegible,
and the text is incomparably better than that
of the Curetonian.

From the day that Cureton's text was in
the hands of scholars the term " Western Text "
became ludicrously inappropriate. It practically
is now used to cover all readings which were
not distinctively approved by texts current in
Alexandria about A.D. 250, or at Antioch a
century later. In fact, it includes all ancient
unrevised texts, so that it is from among the
so-called "Western" variants that we may expect
to find what is true and original. No two
points in Christendom were more isolated from
each other than Edessa in the Euphrates valley
and Carthage in Roman Africa ; it has yet to

be proved that any literary intercourse passed
between them in early times; no two places in
the Empire were less exposed to the universal
solvent of Greek culture.[1] With the aid of Codex
Bobiensis (*k*) and the quotations of St. Cyprian
we can form some idea of the text of the
Gospels as read in North Africa by the middle of
the third century; with the aid of the Sinai
Palimpsest, supplemented by Cureton's MS.,
we can reconstruct the text of the Gospels as
read in the Euphrates valley about the end of
the second century. The agreement of these
two sources brings us back almost to the time
when the Four Gospels first obtained their
canonical position; and where Edessa and
Carthage differ, we may call in the witness of
the text of Alexandria to determine which of
the two has preserved the ancient reading, and
which presents us with the merely local variation.

It was necessary to define our position with
regard to the chief manuscripts and versions,
but, after all, such questions are of the nature
of scaffolding. Of more concern to the reader
of the New Testament are the variations themselves, their nature and their extent. Variations

---

[1] Edessa was first annexed to the Roman Empire in A.D. 216.

of reading are of two kinds, those that were originally accidental and those which were originally intentional. Accidental variations arise from the mistakes of scribes or the mutilation of MSS. For instance, in Mark xv 8 the multitude "cry aloud" to Pilate according to the Authorised Version, but according to the Revised Version they "went up" to him ; the former represents ΑΝΑΒΟΗϹΑϹ, the latter represents ΑΝΑΒΑϹ, and the variation was evidently caused by the similarity of these Greek words. But only a small proportion of the various readings in the New Testament are of this kind. In later times the words were too familiar to be mistaken, though we may remark in passing that a few early "Western" MSS., and notably that Codex Bobiensis about which I have already spoken, are full of very curious blunders. But by far the greater number of the variants were the result of intentional changes of the text. Thus the omission or retention of the Doxology to the Lord's Prayer, or of the episode of the Angel at the Pool, or the substitution of "alms" for "righteousness" in the Sermon on the Mount, cannot have been accidental. Changes such as these were evi-

dently made on purpose, and it is the chief task
of the textual critic to find out when and where
they were made.

We need not here concern ourselves about
the smaller corruptions. These have no doubt
crept in at various times, and have sensibly
impoverished the text and obscured its history.
At the same time the general sense is for the
most part unaltered. The really important
thing is the presence of a whole series of
passages containing fresh matter, which, if not
genuine, must have been derived from sources
independent of our Four Gospels. The longest
and most famous of these Interpolations (for
such I will at once call them for convenience
sake) is the Story of the Woman taken in
Adultery (John vii 53–viii 11). Others,
hardly less notable, are the Bloody Sweat in
the Garden (Luke xxii 43, 44), the prayer
" Father, forgive them " (Luke xxiii 34*a*), and
the word to the Pharisees about the Face of
the Sky (Matt. xvi 2*b*, 3). But not all of the
passages of which I am speaking were taken
up into the later ecclesiastical editions and so
found their way at length into our Authorised
Version ; about half the number failed to get

in, and are now only to be found in a few
ancient and erratic MSS., such as the Cambridge
Codex Bezae (D).   Thus we have the story of
a Light appearing from the Jordan at the
Baptism of our Lord inserted after Matt. iii 16,
and of a Light appearing at the moment of
the Resurrection inserted before Mark xvi 4.
We have a long passage inserted at the end of
Matt. xx 28 after our Lord's rebuke to James
and John, beginning "But ye, seek ye from
little to increase and [not] from greater to
become less";[1] this is followed by the advice
to take the lowest seats, much as in Luke xiv
8–10, but with different wording.   Again, after
Mark xiii 2 (" *There shall not be left one stone in
the Temple that shall not be thrown down* ") we
find added " And after three days another
shall be raised without hands."

Now the first thing to notice about this
whole series of passages is the nature of the
MS. authority by which they are really sup-
ported.   As I have said, a certain number of
them are familiar.   The Greek MSS. from the

[1] The Curetonian Syriac (probably by conjecture) alone
inserts the indispensable " not," which is left out in all the
Greek and Latin authorities for the saying.

fifth century onward, and the great Revised Versions of East and West (the Syriac Peshitta and the Latin Vulgate), all contain some of them, and it would be almost impossible to extract from such authorities the clue to the place where they originally appeared. But as we trace the texts current in various regions to their earlier forms we learn something more. These passages were not part of the Four Gospels as originally current in the East, for they are entirely absent from the Sinai Palimpsest, the oldest and best representative of the texts current in the Euphrates valley. They are not part of the Gospel in the earliest purely Greek text to which we have access, for they are absent from the text approved by Origen and his school ; nor are they quoted by Clement of Alexandria, though this latter circumstance may be the result of accident. But in the real West the case is wholly different. Here the " Interpolations " are at home. They are all attested by some ancient Latin evidence ; even in Africa, where so many later corruptions never penetrated, these longer passages seem to have had a place in the vernacular Bible. The Bobbio fragments (*k*), so far as they are extant, contain them all, and the accurate St. Cyprian himself quotes several of the passages.

We learn therefore that they belong of right to the Gospel as current in the West, and that the Eastern MSS. which contain some of them have ultimately borrowed them from the West. Some have taken more, some less, but had they been original in the East we should have had some right to expect to find evidence there for the whole series ; but that evidence we do not find.   To take only the most striking instance, there is in the East no certain trace of the Story of the Woman taken in Adultery before the middle of the sixth century.

The nearest approach to an Eastern document containing most of the Interpolations is the *Diatessaron*, a Harmony of the Four Gospels into one continuous narrative, which had a great popularity among Syriac-speaking Christians in the third and fourth centuries. But this work, as we are expressly told, was compiled by one Tatian, who was a disciple of Justin Martyr, and had lived and taught many years in Rome.   Tatian only revisited his native country at the end of his career, bringing with him no doubt his *Diatessaron*, already

made from the text current in the West. Yet
this Harmony by no means attests all the
Interpolations : for instance, it contains neither
the passage about the Angel at the Pool nor the
Story of the Woman taken in Adultery.

The modern science of textual criticism is
not only a machine to enable the student to
construct a text of the New Testament which
shall be complete, correct, and free from interpolations ; it aims at being much more. It
aims, as I said earlier in the Lecture, at re-
constructing the history of the book studied ;
and I have not taken you through this rather
dry track merely to reject more intelligently
certain passages out of the Gospels which the
text or margin of the Revised Version have
already for twenty years proclaimed to be
doubtful. But the discovery of the Syriac MS.
of the Gospels at Sinai—for it is mainly that
—has changed the character of the evidence
against them. Before that discovery I could
not have told you with any confidence that the
Interpolations of which I have been speaking
were so decidedly of Western origin, Western
I mean in the true geographical sense, nor
indeed could I have been quite so certain that

they were interpolations, because it would not have been so certain that they all formed part of the same series. But as the Sinai Palimpsest rejects them all as emphatically as does Dr. Hort himself, they all stand or fall together. And as a series they cannot stand, for they include the Story of the Woman taken in Adultery. That beautiful story may very well be true, and we may be well content that under whatever conditions it has found a place in our Bibles, but it was certainly not committed to writing by the author of the Fourth Gospel, nor has it been inserted at an appropriate place. Indeed we may safely say that it would not occur to any one independently to insert it where it is; therefore, and this is the important conclusion to which I want to draw your attention, all the MSS. which contain it must ultimately have drawn it from a common source.[1]   The same is true of some of the other interpolations. A new fact about the Baptism or the Passion must of course be placed in the stories of the Baptism or of the Passion, but there are usually three Gospels to choose from. Yet the interpolation about the Light at

[1] See Note I at the end of these Lectures.

the Baptism is exclusively associated with St. Matthew's Gospel, while on the other hand the quotation at the Baptism of Ps. ii 7 (*Thou art my Son, this day have I begotten Thee*), a various reading which seems also to belong to the series, is only found in MSS. of St. Luke.

The ultimate source, therefore, of all these additions to the narrative is not floating tradition or a non-canonical document, but a single interpolated edition of the Four Gospels themselves. Very likely they were gathered by the editor from tradition or some lost book, and they may indeed have been originally inserted by him in the margin as illustrations of the text. But the fixed position of the interpolations in such documents as do insert them proves that it is from a glossed edition of the Four Gospels that the extra matter has been derived. We are, in a word, in the presence of a very early specimen of Christian study of the Gospels as a single whole. The glossed edition is apparently as old as Justin Martyr, certainly as old as Tatian, *i.e.* we may put it at latest about the middle of the second century. It belongs to the West, and there is no name to whom we have any solid reason to assign it, but the learning it shows is extensive, and we can hardly be far wrong if we suppose the editor to have lived himself in Rome, the great Western centre of Christianity.

It has been generally conjectured from a passage in Eusebius (*H.E.* iii 39 *ad fin.*) that the Story of the Woman taken in Adultery was quoted from the lost *Gospel according to the Hebrews* by Papias of Hierapolis about 150 A.D. Papias's five books of Expositions of the Oracles of the Lord may therefore have been the source whence most of these additions to our Gospels were taken.[1]

What, however, I want to leave most on your minds is that the work of the textual critics of our generation has revealed the existence of this interpolated edition of the Gospels as a definite literary work, which by its very existence shows that the Four Gospels were already collected together about A.D. 150.

---

[1] Some of the passages might very well have been taken from the Gospel of the Hebrews itself, but others could not have been so derived : in such cases as the story of the Angel at the Pool, or the saying *Ye know not what spirit ye are of* (added to Luke ix 54), the additions are part of the particular narrative in hand, and therefore represent a tradition gathering round the Lord's words. This again suggests the work of Papias.

The Gospels as separate works are yet older, but this interpolated edition is, I think, the earliest witness to their existence as the four volumes of a Canon. It may indeed have been the earliest gathering together of our Four Gospels into one exclusive series, just as Tatian's Harmony, its contemporary, was the last attempt to construct a Gospel which should supersede those in use.

We have glanced at the earliest evidence for the Canon of the Gospels : in the next Lecture I hope to say something about their composition and the sources from which they seem to be derived. But before we leave the department connected with the text I must not altogether pass over the most important variation of all, viz. the omission or retention of the " last twelve verses " of St. Mark's Gospel. This is all the more necessary, as the discussion of the question leads up to the subject of the Gospel of Peter, a document long lost, of which a large fragment has come to light within the memory of all of us.

But first as to the facts about the conclusion to the Gospel of St. Mark. You will find the disputed verses marked off from the rest in the Revised Version. At xvi 8 the women at the Sepulchre on Easter morning have just seen the empty grave and the young man in the white robe, who tells them that Jesus the Nazarene is risen from the dead and will go before them to Galilee : they are terrified and hasten away from the tomb, and say nothing to any one for their fright. . . . Here the narrative is suddenly broken off and the twelve verses in dispute follow. They do not go on about the frightened women, but starting afresh from the Resurrection itself, they mention the appearances of the Lord to Mary Magdalene, to the two disciples in the country (as in St. Luke), to the eleven as they sat at meat (again as in St. Luke), and then follows the final charge to the apostles.

The disputed verses were omitted in the Origenian text, represented by ℵ and B, though there are indications that the scribe of these MSS. knew that the text was imperfect. It is of far more importance that the verses are also omitted in the Syriac Palimpsest at Sinai, the beginning of St. Luke following Mark xvi 8 on the same column, with only such a space between as was needed for the colophon and title. This is all the more striking and unexpected, because Tatian's *Diatessaron*, the Harmony of the Gospels which was so popular in the Syriac-speaking Church, certainly contained the verses ; but we have seen that the Syriac *Diatessaron* is not altogether free from readings which belong properly to the West. The African Latin, as represented by the invaluable Codex Bobiensis (*k*), takes a third course. It does not contain the disputed verses, but in their place puts another ending thus : [1] *Now they* [*i.e.* the women] *when they came out from the tomb fled, for fright and terror held them on account of their fear. Now all the things which they had been commanded, to them also that were with Peter they shortly declared ; afterwards Jesus himself also appeared, and from the East even unto the West sent by them the holy and uncorrupted preaching of eternal salvation. Amen.*

This same shorter conclusion is also found in a number of MSS. mostly connected with Egypt, but except in the ancient Latin MS. just quoted it is always found in conjunction with the longer conclusion as one of two alternatives.

It is the witness of the Sinaitic Syriac and

[1] I pass over one or two clerical errors, such as this MS. presents on every page.

the Latin Codex Bobiensis which irretrievably condemn the disputed verses at the end of St. Mark, for the short conclusion to the Gospel which I have just read out is obviously an attempt to supply some sort of ending to the incomplete sentence in verse 8. That the Gospel was originally intended to finish at verse 8 is quite inconceivable. Not only the narrative, the paragraph, and the sentence are each left incomplete, but even the subordinate clause seems to hang in the air. Greek sentences do not usually finish off with a particle, and the two last words ἐφοβοῦντο γὰρ . . . may very well have meant "for they were afraid of" *something* now lost, whether it was the chief Priests or the fanatical mob or the incredulous and mournful scorn of St. Peter and his companions. The Gospel as we have it is accidentally imperfect, not intentionally curtailed ; in other words, the MS. from which all our copies are derived must have lost one or more leaves at the end.

The general agreement of our first two Gospels throughout the history of the Passion would make it antecedently probable that the genuine Gospel according to St. Mark, the

Gospel as it left its author's hands, would pro-
ceed upon the lines of the conclusion to St.
Matthew. There the main fact related is that
the eleven disciples went into Galilee and saw the
Lord in the mountain in Galilee, where He gives
them His last commands. This is therefore
what we should expect in the genuine Gospel
of Mark, and our expectation has been remark-
ably confirmed by the fragment of the long-lost
Gospel according to Peter, which was discovered
in a tomb at Akhmim in Egypt and published
in 1892.

The Gospel of Peter had long been known
to scholars by name. Eusebius, in his *Church
History*, in this as in so much else our chief
source of information, tells us [1] that it used to be
read in the Church of a place called Rhossus
near Antioch. Serapion, Bishop of Antioch at
the end of the second century, had at first not
forbidden this practice, but afterwards he found
that the document was used to establish the
heretical doctrines of the Docetae, and so he
ordered it to be discontinued. Docetae, as you
are probably aware, was the name given to
those who held that the sufferings of Christ, or

[1] Eusebius, *H.E.* vi 12.

even His visible body, were not real, but only in appearance; accordingly, in the newly-recovered fragment, we read that when the Lord was crucified *He kept silence as having no pain* (*Ev. Petri*, § 4), the Greek ὡς μηδὲν πόνον ἔχων meaning equally well "as if He had no pain," or "seeing that He had no pain."

The fragment recovered in 1892 contains the Passion story from Pilate's washing his hands to the Resurrection. In the main it follows the familiar lines; indeed many scholars are convinced that the author knew of and used all our canonical Four Gospels. In any case there are almost certain indications of the use of St. Mark's Gospel in the account of the visit of the women to the sepulchre. We read : " And at dawn upon the Lord's day Mary Magdalen, a disciple of the Lord, [who] fearing because of the Jews, since they were burning with wrath, had not done at the Lord's sepulchre the things which the women are wont to do for those that die and are beloved by them, took her friends with her and came to the sepulchre where He was laid. And they feared lest the Jews should see them, and they said ' Even if on that day on which He was crucified we

could not weep and lament, yet now let us do
these things at His sepulchre. But who shall
roll away for us the stone that is laid at the
door of the sepulchre, that we may enter in and
sit by Him and do the things that are due?
For the stone was great, and we fear lest some
one see us. And even if we cannot, yet let us
set at the door the things which we bring for a
memorial of Him ; let us weep and lament,
until we come unto our home.' And they
went away and found the tomb opened, and
coming near they looked in there ; and they
see there a certain young man sitting in
the midst of the tomb, beautiful and clothed in
a very bright robe ; who said to them, ' Why are
ye come ? whom seek ye ? Is it that crucified
One ? He is risen and gone away. But
if ye believe not, look in and see the place where
He lay, that He is not [here] ; for He is risen
and gone away thither, whence He was sent.'
Then the women feared and fled.

" Now it was the last day of the unleavened
bread, and many went forth returning to their
homes, as the feast was ended. But we, the
twelve disciples of the Lord, wept and were
grieved : and each one grieving for that which

was come to pass departed to his home. But I, Simon Peter, and Andrew my brother took our nets and went away to the sea ; and there was with us Levi the son of Alphaeus, whom the Lord . . ."[1]

Here the fragment comes to an abrupt conclusion, and the glimpse of our Lord manifested to these apostles, which the Gospel of Peter no doubt went on to narrate, must remain for us undescribed until a fresh MS. of the Gospel of Peter be discovered. It has been often supposed that the lost scene in Galilee would prove to be a reminiscence of the last chapter of the Fourth Gospel, but *Levi the son of Alphaeus* is not mentioned in that Gospel, while he is mentioned in St. Mark's Gospel, and by this name in St. Mark alone.[2] Now when we consider that in all the long extract which I have just read to you the Gospel of Peter follows what remains of the genuine part of Mark xvi ; and then, when the text of St. Mark as known to us fails, goes on with a narrative about Galilee, in which the name of an apostle

[1] *Ev. Petri*, §§ 12-14 : I have followed Canon Armitage Robinson's translation.

[2] Mark ii 14.

is given in the form characteristic of St. Mark, I think we are not pressing conjecture too far if we gather that the author of the Gospel of Peter knew and used our Gospel according to St. Mark in its original form before it had lost its last leaves.

What inferences, then, can we draw from the state in which the last chapter of St. Mark's Gospel has come down to us? The first and chief inference I have already stated. Since the Gospel breaks off at xvi 8 in the middle of a dependent clause, the mutilation must have been originally accidental ; all our copies, therefore, are ultimately descended from a single imperfect copy, which had lost its last leaf.[1] But we can go one step further yet. A Gospel which survives in a single imperfect copy must have been, at least for a time, out of fashion. Now, as we shall see in the next Lecture, St. Mark's Gospel appears to be the earliest of the four, and to have been the foundation upon which other Gospels, especially

---

[1] A "last leaf" implies a MS. in the form of a book rather than a roll. It is uncertain when the book form first made its appearance, but it is noteworthy that all the very ancient *Christian* papyri (such as the Oxyrhynchus St. John, etc.) have been books, not rolls.

our Gospel according to St. Matthew, were constructed. The later Gospels, no doubt, reflected the wants and the tastes of their first public, or they would never have been published at all, and the mutilated conclusion of St. Mark tells us of a period — shall we say the first quarter of the second century?—when the only copy of that Gospel which was destined to survive was lying neglected and forgotten in the tiny library of some early Christian, perhaps at Rome, perhaps at Alexandria. Then came the time when the spread of unauthorised beliefs and new philosophies among Christian people made it necessary for the churches to choose out which of the evangelical narratives were to be accepted by the newer generation that was growing up. Of this vitally important moment in the history of the books of the New Testament we know next to nothing. Possibly the action of the Church was quickened by the example of Marcion, the anti-Semite heresiarch, whose Bible consisted of the Gospel of St. Luke as altered to suit his own views, together with most of the Epistles of St. Paul. The exact reasons which led to the inclusion of the Gospel according to St. Mark in the

Church's Canon we do not know, but it is not unlikely that the traditional connexion of the work with St. Peter was an important considera- tion. But inclusion in the Canon could not bring back the lost ending, and our Second Gospel remains to-day, like so many of the most precious examples of ancient art, mutilated at the extremity. As part of the four-fold Gospel Canon, a new lease of existence, happily for us, was assured to it ; but it had entered into life maimed.

LECTURE II

QUARTI EUANGELIORUM · IOHANNIS EX DECIPOLIS
COHORTANTIBUS CONDESCIPULIS ET EPS SUIS
DIXIT CONIEIUNATE MIHI · ODIE TRIDUO ET QUID
CUIQUE FUERIT REUELATUM ALTERUTRUM
NOBIS ENNAREMUS   EADEM NOCTE REUE
LATUM ANDREAE EX APOSTOLIS UT RECOGNIS
CENTIBUS CUNTIS IOHANNIS SUO NOMINE
CUNTA DISCRIBRET

Muratorian Canon.

.

THE GOSPELS AS SEPARATE WORKS

(1) *The Synoptic Gospels*

WE come now to perhaps the most important
and fascinating literary problem in the world,
namely, the composition and origin of our four
Gospels. In speaking of what is usually called
textual criticism, we practically treat the four
Gospels as a single whole; they are, for the
most part, written continuously in the same
MS., one after the other. We are, in fact,
tracing the history of the ecclesiastical edition
of the collected volume of the Canon. But
that is not the first stage. Each Gospel is
really a separate work, designed for separate
circulation. They are not independent; the
later ones knew of and used the earlier, but in
design they were intended either to stand alone

or (as in the case of St. Luke's Gospel) to form
the first volume of a longer historical work.

The only very early pieces of information
which have come down to us about the composition of the first three Gospels are the
enigmatic remarks quoted by Eusebius from
Papias, who was bishop of Hierapolis about
the middle of the second century. He says
that "Matthew collected together the *Logia*
(*i.e.* the Oracles) in the Hebrew language, and
each interpreted them as he could"; and he
also makes a statement to the effect that Mark,
as the interpreter of Peter, wrote down accurately, though not in order.[1] If I were to
attempt to give you an account of what has
been written on these statements during the
present century, it would take up not one, but
half a dozen lectures. Like the oracles of
Matthew, each scholar has interpreted them as
he could, but, in so doing, the world has become
very little the wiser. The information given is
not explicit enough to form the basis of our
main theories. One thing, at least, is clear.
Our present Gospel according to Matthew is
not, as it stands, a translation from the Hebrew,

[1] Eusebius, *H.E.* iii 39.

so that the words of Papias cannot refer directly to that work.

Comparatively little real progress was made in the study of the mutual relations of the Gospels while this inquiry was undertaken more as a question of theology than as a matter of literary criticism. I am not speaking only of apologists and conservative scholars. It is true that from the days of St. Augustine the Gospel which bears the name of St. Mark has met with a certain amount of depreciation. It does not even profess to be the direct composition of an apostle ; it could not be supposed that St. Matthew would need to use the work of one who was not an eye-witness, and it was generally held that our Second Gospel was a compilation of the Gospels of Matthew and Luke, supplemented by details which St. Mark might have learned by intercourse with St. Peter. The curious thing is that this prejudice was shared by the dominant school of advanced criticism fifty years ago. St. Mark's Gospel is neither specifically Jewish Christian nor Pauline ; moreover, it does not give the Sermon on the Mount, and those who felt that the Sermon on the Mount presented the most faithful picture of the earliest Christian doctrine were unwilling to regard St. Mark's Gospel as a primary source. The Tübingen critics especially decried it, regarding it as a mere epitome of our First and Third Gospels, made in the middle of the second century, in the days of Justin Martyr. But they never gave any satisfactory explanation why this late compilation was entirely unprovided with a story of the Nativity, the details of which, as recorded in Matthew and Luke, Justin Martyr is so fond of illustrating from prophecy.

The first great advance, in my opinion, was marked by the publication of Mr. Rushbrooke's *Synopticon* in 1880. This work gives in parallel columns the Greek text of St. Mark with the corresponding passages from St. Matthew and St. Luke: what is common to all three is printed in red, and the words common to Matthew and Mark, or Luke and Mark, or Matthew and Luke, are distinguished by separate types. At the end of the book the parts of Matthew and Luke which have no parallel in Mark are given separately. It was possible therefore for the reader to see at a glance how matters stood between these three Gospels.

Synopticon had been designed to illustrate the theories of Dr. E. A. Abbott, author of the article " Gospels " in the *Encyclopaedia Britannica* (9th edition) ; four years later, in 1884, an English version of it, with an introduction by Dr. Abbott and Mr. Rushbrooke, was issued under the title of *The Common Tradition of the Synoptic Gospels.* This is the little work which I recommended for those attending these Lectures, not because the special theory of Dr. Abbott is particularly convincing, but because it provides us with the materials for our study so admirably arranged.

Last year a book called *Horae Synopticae,* by the Rev. Sir John Caesar Hawkins, came out at Oxford. It contains very careful analyses of the peculiar phraseology and literary usage of each several Gospel, together with notes on the passages which throw most light on their relations to one another. It modestly calls itself " Contributions to the study of the Synoptic Problem," but I do not know of any work in English or German which puts the complicated question more clearly.

The three Gospels, according to Matthew, Mark, and Luke, obviously have something in

common : they must either copy one another
or make use of a common source. The first
question is whether this source or sources be
written or oral. My own opinion, most unhesitatingly, is that it was a written source.
For in the first place the common matter was
not some floating tradition, the property of all
the Christian community, or of all the community of a certain place. Had it been this,
I cannot but think that the incidents identically
related by Matthew, Mark, and Luke would
have been to a larger extent the critical points
of our Lord's ministry, and not a capricious
selection of anecdotes. The story of the
Resurrection, the words from the Cross, the
narrative of the Last Supper—in these we
might have expected all our authorities to
agree, even in detail ; but they do not agree.
On the other hand, the parenthesis explaining
that Christ turned from addressing the Pharisees
to say to the sick of the palsy " Arise " is found
in all three Synoptic Gospels ; all three insert
the statement concerning Herod's alarm about
Jesus at the same point, and Matthew and
Mark further go on to relate, so to speak in a
footnote, the circumstances of John the Baptist's

murder ; all three inform us that the Pharisees
in framing their question about the tribute-
money hypocritically assured our Lord that He
taught the way of God in truth.   These points
are quite individual ; an oral tradition which
contained them must be held to have had
singular consistency.   I am not denying the
retentive capacity of Oriental memories, so often
invoked by the defenders of an oral hypothesis ;
but if our evangelists had worked upon a fixed
oral tradition of this definite sort, I cannot
imagine why they dared to take such liberties
. with it.   A definite oral tradition is authorita-
tive : can we conceive of an oral tradition which
accurately distinguishes between the *baskets*
(κόφινοι) of fragments taken up after the
feeding of the 5000 and the *hampers* (σφυρίδες)
taken up after feeding the 4000, but which
left the details of the Crucifixion and the
Resurrection vague ?

A written source, on the other hand, is
perfectly definite but not necessarily authorita-
tive.   Where the evangelists simply copy their
common source they agree, whether the point
of agreement be important or not, while at the
same time the existence of the written document

did not prevent the use of other documents or any oral information which might be to hand. There was nothing to compel either of our Evangelists to follow exactly the documents upon which they worked : if they had had such respect for their predecessors' work as never to alter it, they would never have dared to supersede these documents or traditions by their own new Gospels. They would have been mere scribes, or at the most harmonists like Tatian.

But we can go further. In the parts common to Mark, Matthew, and Luke there is a good deal in which all three verbally agree ; there is also much common to Mark and Matthew and much common to Mark and Luke, but hardly anything common to Matthew and Luke which Mark does not also share. Moreover, there is very little of Mark which is not more or less adequately represented in either Matthew or Luke. In other words, Mark contains the whole of the document which Matthew and Luke have independently used.

This conclusion is extremely important ; it is the one solid contribution which the scholar-

ship of the nineteenth century has made
towards the solution of the Synoptic problem.
No doubt the matter requires reflection, as Dr.
Abbott remarks, but there is no escape from
the logic of his singularly lucid statement. For
how else could it happen that Mark contains
all that is common to Matthew and Luke? If
we assumed that Mark borrowed from Matthew
and Luke, " Mark could only have achieved
such a result *by carefully underlining all the
words common to Matthew's and Luke's narratives*, and by then writing a narrative of his
own, which should *include all these words* and
yet preserve the natural style of an original
composition. The difficulty of doing this is
enormous, and will be patent to any one who
will try to perform a similar literary feat himself.
To embody *the whole* of even one document in
a narrative of one's own without copying it
verbatim, and to do this in a free and natural
manner, requires no little care ; but to take
two documents, to put them side by side and
analyse their common matter, and then to
write a narrative, graphic, abrupt, and in all
respects the opposite of artificial, which shall
contain every word that is common to both—

this would be a *tour de force* even for a skilful literary forger of these days, and may be dismissed as an impossibility for the writer of the Second Gospel." [1]

So far Dr. Abbott ; but at this point I must part company with him. I do not believe that any document underlies the Second Gospel, for I cannot but think that the document which the First and Third Evangelists have independently used is St. Mark's Gospel itself.

Dr. Abbott believed in an original document, written in a short, abrupt style, so abrupt as to be obscure, underlying the three Synoptic Gospels. The differences in their common narratives arose, according to this theory, from the different ways in which our three evangelists interpreted this original document. Other scholars imagine an *Ur-Marcus*, as they say in Germany, *i.e.* an earlier form, out of which our Second Gospel was compiled. But the objection remains that a theory of successive editions of what is recognisably the Gospel according to St. Mark presupposes a great amount of interest in the circle of ideas and events with which that Gospel chiefly concerns itself, and that

[1] *Common Tradition of the Synoptic Gospels*, p. 7.

interest does not appear. In the extant
remains of very early Christian literature we
find the doctrines of the Crucifixion and the
Resurrection ; we find the arguments from
prophecy ; we find the ethical teaching of the
Sermon on the Mount ; we also find in such
writers as Justin Martyr copious references to
the story of the Nativity, as related by St.
Matthew and St. Luke. But the details of
the Galilean Ministry are hardly mentioned.
It is not a mere chance that the two non-
canonical Gospel fragments discovered in recent
years—the Oxyrhynchus *Logia* and the Gospel
of Peter—concern themselves, the one with
detached sayings of Christ, the other with
the Passion.[1] It is the peculiar merit of St. Mark's
Gospel, from the point of view of the historical
investigator, that it deals with a cycle of events
quite foreign to the life and interests of the
growing Christian communities.

The probability that the First and Third
Evangelists actually used our Gospel according
to St. Mark is increased when we consider the

[1] The Fayyum Papyrus also is connected with the Passion,
but the surviving fragment is too small for us to form any
certain idea of its real character.

nature of most of its peculiarities. They are
interesting indeed to us, but it is easy to see
that they might once have been thought need-
less or even offensive. It did not help the
preaching of the Gospel to read that our Lord's
relations thought Him mad (iii 21), or to
listen to the twice repeated complaint that He
and His disciples had no time for their meals
(iii 20, vi 31). The story of the young man
who followed Christ when the apostles fled is
absolutely pointless (xiv 51, 52). As Sir John
Hawkins says (*Horae Synopticae*, p. 182) : " So
far as we can judge from our earliest records,
'the memoirs of the Apostles' were chiefly
drawn upon for the purpose of (i.) exhibiting
'Jesus of Nazareth' as 'approved of God by
mighty works and wonders and signs' (Acts ii
22) ; and (ii.) of supplying accounts of his
teaching, especially on moral subjects (see, *e.g.*,
Rom. xii, James iv, Clem. Rom. xiii ; *Ep.
Polycarp.* ii, *Didache* i). There would be no
materials available for these purposes, nor again
for the proofs of the Messiahship of Jesus
drawn from prophecy for Jewish hearers, nor
again for the articles of the Creed which soon
began to grow out of the baptismal confession

of faith, in the very great majority of these Marcan augmentations."

We of the nineteenth century approach the Gospel history with different, though it may be with not less reverent, eyes. These unimportant, undignified details are valuable to us not only for their picturesqueness and simplicity, but also as giving us a much needed assurance that the Evangelist is in vital connection with the scenes that he describes. I am not here pressing the absolute historicity of the Second Gospel. It does not profess to have been compiled by an eye-witness, and a generation and a half of most tremendous change, spiritual and political, had passed between the events and the telling of the tale. But we are still in the region of history. Our Lord and His contemporaries are still real persons ; they have not faded into symbols.

The Christians of the second century did not care for local colour. Of all the four canonical Gospels that according to Matthew is most quoted in the second century, and the literary methods of its compiler excellently indicate the prevailing taste of the age. He has taken the historical framework from St.

Mark, but he tones down the narrative, and abridges it to make room for his illustrations from Old Testament prophecy, for his story of the Infancy, and, above all, for his reports of our Lord's longer sayings, many of which are also found in St. Luke's Gospel. It is generally conjectured that this invaluable collection of sayings was taken by St. Luke and by the compiler of the First Gospel from the " Oracles," which (as Papias informs us) the apostle St. Matthew collected together in the " Hebrew " language. This is the document usually called by modern writers the *Logia*, from the expression used by Papias. Of course, this conjectural work of St. Matthew is irretrievably lost, along with the rest of the Semitic literature of the earliest Christianity, and opinions differ widely as to its contents and arrangement. It is perhaps safe to say that it included something which was recognisably the Sermon on the Mount, *i.e.* a collection of sayings, beginning with Beatitudes, and ending with the simile of the men that built their houses, one on the rock and the other on the sand (*cf.* Matt. v-vii ; Luke vi 20-49). Besides detached sayings such as these, it seems to have included

stories which led up to remarkable words of
Christ, such as that of the Centurion's boy
(Matt. viii 5-13 ; Luke vii 2-10). But it can
hardly have included the story of the Passion,
as otherwise it is difficult to explain why our
Gospel according to Matthew should follow
St. Mark so closely in the last three chapters.
St. Luke, it may be remarked, does follow, in
the main, an independent story of the Passion,
and only uses St. Mark in the last three
chapters as a secondary source for single
details.   This was but what we might reasonably have expected ; the thing was not done
in a corner, and it is not wonderful that more
than one account of it survived to later times.
It is otherwise with the earlier Galilean Ministry,
the tale of which few were ever in a position
to tell (Acts i 22, 23).   It may not be out of
place to point out that the great historical dis-
tinction between St. Luke's Passion story and
St. Mark's is that, according to the genuine St.
Mark, as represented by Matt. xxviii and the
" Gospel of Peter," the appearances of Christ to
the disciples after the Resurrection take place
in Galilee, while, according to St. Luke, they
occur at or near Jerusalem.

But the consideration of these things lies rather outside our present subject. We must now turn to some questions connected with the origin of the Fourth Gospel, the Gospel according to St. John.

(2) *The Fourth Gospel*

During the present century a great deal has been written about the authorship and historical character of the Fourth Gospel. The question is a very delicate literary problem, because we are not dealing with a mass of popular traditions, or with documents which reflect popular traditions, but with the expression of some of the deeper thoughts of a great mind. This is the case whether the Gospel be St. John's or not, whether it accurately reports the words of our Lord or only tells us what a later disciple thought He must have said. Such a question demands more than reverence and erudition : it demands also literary tact and knowledge of literature and the habit of just literary criticism. Very few have approached the subject endowed with the necessary qualifications, and for my own part I have found Matthew Arnold's remarks in *God and the Bible*, chaps. v and vi, to be much the most illuminating investigation of the origin and character of the Gospel according to St. John which has yet appeared. That distinguished poet and critic, in his book *Literature and Dogma*, had quoted out of the' Fourth Gospel certain sayings as the genuine teaching of Jesus, and for this he had been taken to task by some of the advanced critical school. His reply (in *God and the Bible*) is mainly concerned with defending the existence of this genuine element in the Fourth Gospel, and explaining how it came to be there in the midst of what he unhesitatingly rejected.

It is now the fashion among literary people to deplore Matthew Arnold's incursions into biblical criticism. He is often supposed to have rushed in as a kind of dilettante theological amateur into regions where none but professors and clergymen should adventure themselves. The fact is that most people, especially most literary people, do not know how well equipped he was for the work. He had the habit and experience of literary criticism, and an excellent knowledge not only of the works of modern theologians, but—what is of much more importance—of the ancient sources also. Few professed theologians know how to quote as well as Matthew Arnold from Eusebius or the *Philosophumena*.

Those of you who have read the chapters in question will notice to what a great extent his view of the Fourth Gospel is based upon the earlier traditions about it. When all is said and done the Christian Church has had a certain continuity, and it is unlikely that no trustworthy detail of the first appearance of this great work should survive. It is not as if the Fourth Gospel was a product of the far-off, primitive, Semitic Christianity of Palestine. On the contrary, it is undoubtedly a document written in Greek, and the Church tradition tells us that it was not written till the end of St. John's life, at the close of the first century of our era. St. Polycarp, bishop of Smyrna, who was martyred in A.D. 155 or 156 at the age of 86, is said to have been a disciple of St. John, and St. Polycarp in turn was known to St. Irenaeus, to whom the absolute canonicity of all our Four Gospels was a fixed dogma. The chasm therefore in our knowledge is short, and the links of the chain connecting St. Iraeneus with St. John are few.

At the same time the witness actually borne by St. Polycarp to the Johannine writings is very peculiar. We have a letter of his, written about a quarter of a century after the traditional date of the Gospel, and we have the prayer which he is said to have prayed at the stake. But we find no quotation from the Fourth Gospel, though in the epistle there are clear parallels to the Synoptic Gospels, and in the prayer St. Polycarp gives thanks that he had been found worthy to partake of the cup of Christ, *i.e.* the cup of martyrdom, which (as the Gospels according to Mark and Matthew tell us) it was promised that St. John should drink. It is always hazardous to argue from silence, but this absence of testimony in a quarter where we might reasonably have expected it is remarkable, and has never been explained by those who regard the Fourth Gospel as having enjoyed unquestioned authority in Asia Minor, its own birthplace, from very early times.

What we do find in St. Polycarp is a certain similarity of phraseology with the Johannine writings. He says (*Ep. ad Phil.* vii): " For whosoever doth not acknowledge Jesus Christ to have come in the flesh is antichrist, and

whosoever doth not acknowledge the witness of
the cross is of the devil, and whosoever per-
verteth the oracles of the Lord (μεθοδεύῃ τὰ
λόγια τοῦ κυρίου) to his own desires and saith
there is neither resurrection nor judgment, he
is the first-born of Satan." [1]　This conception
of "antichrist," and the phrase "Jesus Christ
come in the flesh," both belong to that circle of
ideas represented in the New Testament by the
Johannine writings, and by them alone.

The witness of the *Didache* is somewhat
similar to that of St. Polycarp, and is probably
of about the same date.　This exceedingly
valuable document was published for the first
time in 1883.　It is an early Christian law-
book, giving the rules of conduct and of govern-
ment for the Church.　No doubt some of the
precepts are based on older, perhaps pre-
Christian, materials, but even in its present
form it seems to date from the middle of the
second century.　The eucharistic prayers en-
joined in it are particularly interesting : it may

---

[1] " First-born of Satan " was St. Polycarp's name for
Marcion (Iren. *Haer.* iii 4), and it is to Marcion's doctrine, or
rather to that of his predecessors, that reference here appears to
be made.

be said generally of ancient Liturgies, that the more ancient they are the more they contain parallels to the prayers in the *Didache*. The phraseology of these very early Christian prayers is doubly remarkable: on the one hand, that they speak of our Lord as παῖς θεοῦ, the phrase meaning either *son* or *servant* of God, as in the early chapters of Acts and in St. Polycarp's dying prayer (Eusebius, *H.E.* iv 15); on the other, that they have just the same sort of parallelism that we find in St. Polycarp with the Johannine writings. No doubt the prayers of which I am speaking will be familiar to many of you. You will remember that at consecration first it was said concerning the Cup :—
We thank Thee, our Father, for the holy Vine of David Thy Servant, which Thou hast made known to us through Jesus Thy Servant : to Thee be the glory for ever ! Then concerning the Bread broken :—*We thank Thee, our Father, for the Life and Knowledge which Thou hast made known to us through Jesus Thy Servant : to Thee be the glory for ever ! For as this bread scattered in grains upon the hills and gathered together hath become one loaf, so gather Thy Church from the ends of the earth into Thy*

Kingdom ; for Thine is the glory and the power through Jesus Christ for ever ! And in the prayer after the sacred meal it was said :—*May Grace come and this world pass away !*

The holy Vine of David, the Life and Knowledge made known by Jesus, the spiritual food and drink and eternal Life through Jesus, the passing away of this world (ὁ κόσμος οὗτος), all these are thoroughly Johannine ideas, though it would be hazardous to affirm that their presence in the eucharistic prayers of the *Didache* implies the literary use of the Fourth Gospel. But they do show us that the ideas which find their expression in the Fourth Gospel are not wholly the isolated offspring of a solitary thinker. If, as Church tradition tells us, the apostle John lived to old age at Ephesus, his long presence there must have influenced the Church in Asia. If the Fourth Gospel in any way represents the genuine teaching of Christ as reported through St. John, we cannot imagine that the peculiar cycle of ideas which we find there was otherwise utterly unrepresented in early Christian teaching. The important thing for us is not whether the Fourth Gospel was written by John the son of Zebedee, but whether it truly reports the teaching of our Lord.

The people who fastened on the Fourth Gospel from the first were the early " Gnostic " heretics, the early thinkers who stood on the borderland of Christianity and attempted by its aid to frame a philosophy of the world. And similarly, the people who were the last to receive the Fourth Gospel were some otherwise orthodox folk of Asia Minor, who appear to have been simply conservative and averse to theological speculation. They seem to have been extinct by the fourth century. St. Epiphanius, from whom we hear about them, with his customary courtesy towards those from whom he differed in opinion, because they rejected the doctrine of the Divine Word or *Logos*, calls them " Alogi " —that is to say, *Brute Beasts*, irrational and speechless. Without a word, indeed, they have died out, leaving no writings behind, a circum-stance much to be regretted from the point of view of the historical investigator.

But perhaps the most curious witness to the Fourth Gospel which has turned up in these last few years is that borne by a document known as the *Acts of John*. Some fragments of

this work had long been known, but a large
piece embracing what had been already known,
and more besides, was detected by Dr. M. R.
James in a fourteenth century MS. at Vienna,
and published in 1897. The *Acts of John*
represent that view of Christianity and of Jesus
Christ which is farthest removed of all from
modern thought. To the orthodox Christian
Jesus of Nazareth is very God, and at the same
time true Man ; to the modern agnostic He is a
good man deified by his followers. But to the
author of the *Acts of John* He was not Man at
all. He had no proper shape or body, only an
appearance, and to one person He appeared in
one shape, and to another in a shape totally
different ; even the clothes which He seemed to
be wearing were visionary. God, in fact, had
sent His Word down to men ; symbolically and
by a dispensation He had preached to men for
their conversion and salvation in the form of a
human being.

According to these *Acts* the crucifixion
never really took place. At the time of the
great darkness our Lord appeared to St. John,
who had sought refuge from the Jews in a cave,
and said to him : *John, unto the multitude down*

below in Jerusalem I am being crucified, and
pierced with lances and reeds, and gall and
vinegar is given Me to drink : but unto thee I
am speaking, and hearken thou to what I say.
I put it into thy heart to come up into this
mountain, that thou mightest hear matters needful
for a disciple to learn from his teacher, and for a
man to learn from his God (A.J. xii). Then
follows the mystical teaching about the Cross,
which according to this Gnostic view was the
true significance of the Passion.

To all this teaching the Fourth Gospel is
utterly opposed. It is the Fourth Gospel
which tells us that Christ on the cross thirsted,[1]
it is the Fourth Gospel which asseverates in
the strongest possible manner that the dead
body of the Lord presented all the appearance
of a material human body.[2] It is, in a word,
so much opposed to the teaching of the *Acts of*
John that Dr. Corssen, a distinguished German
scholar, not long ago raised the question
whether the Gospel was not written to contradict
these *Acts.* Since Dr. Corssen wrote we have

[1] John xix 28.
[2] John xix 34, 35. For the view of the author of the
Gospel, see 1 John v 6.

come to know more of the *Acts of John*, and
we see that they are later than the Gospel, and
that they make use of phrases taken from the
Gospel. At the same time the Docetic view
of the person of Christ was prevalent at very
early times, as we know from other sources,
and though the *Acts of John* about which I
have been speaking are later than the Fourth
Gospel, the doctrine of these Acts may well
have been current in certain circles when the
Fourth Gospel was being composed. It is
difficult to resist the inference that the object
of the stress laid upon the piercing of our Lord
on the cross was to assure the readers of the
reality of His body against the Docetae, just as
tradition assures us that the prologue of the
Gospel was written against Cerinthus, who
asserted that Christ never existed before He
was born of Mary.

The author of the *Acts of John*, however,
found a way of reconciling the Gospel with his
own theory. To quote Dr. James (*Apocrypha
Anecdota*, ii. p. 149) : " His notion is that St.
John wrote for the multitude certain comparatively plain and easy episodes in the life of the
Lord, but that to the inner circle of the faithful

his teaching was widely different. In the Gospel and Epistle we have his exoteric teaching ; in the *Acts* his esoteric. . . . Leucius [the reputed author of the *Acts of John*] is writing a commentary upon St. John's narrative, with the view of explaining it all away. . . . The crucifying, the piercing, the blood, the death, were all visible phenomena : only they did not really happen to the Lord. Thus it was right for St. John to record them, but only for the sake of the outer circle. They had their importance as evidence that Christ came into the world, but (and this is the key-note of the whole passage) they were all contrived 'symbolically, and by a dispensation for the converting and saving of men.' "

I have lingered over these *Acts of John* and their relation to the Fourth Gospel, partly because the ground is comparatively unfamiliar, but chiefly because the point of view is so far removed from ours. At the same time this curious document tells us that a devout and reverent Christian, about the middle of the second century, saw no harm in inventing speeches and putting them into the mouth of his Lord. Such a proceeding helps us to

understand how the brief and pregnant words
of Christ came to be amplified into the theological lectures which we read in the Fourth
Gospel. Indeed, the literary methods of Leucius
and of the fourth Evangelist are not dissimilar ;
there are striking ideas, which are repeated
again and again until they almost lose their
effect. And just as it is the singular beauty
and power of some of the original ideas in the
Gospel which makes us feel that they must
have come from some other more profound
Mind than the writer of the Gospel, so there
are one or two very striking words in the *Acts
of John.* Christ says there *I am a Lamp to
thee who beholdest Me, I am a Mirror to thee
who perceivest Me, I am a Door to thee who
knockest at Me, I am a way to thee, a wayfarer.*
Or again, *Who am I ? Thou shalt know when
I go away ; what I am now seen to be, that am I
not, [but what I am] thou shalt see when thou
comest. If thou hadst known how to suffer, thou
wouldst have had the power not to suffer.* All
these sayings recall the sayings of Christ in the
Fourth Gospel, and if any one should say that
they were simply suggested by what we read
in the Fourth Gospel itself, we must in that

case acknowledge that the art of reminting the
words of the Lord was not confined to the four
evangelists.

I regret not to be able to speak more
definitely to you about the composition and
authorship of the Gospel according to St. John.
That we have in it throughout the accurate
report of an eye-witness is surely inconceivable ;
at the same time there are too many indications
that the writer of it had access to genuine
traditions, *i.e.* to the memory of an apostle, for
us to reject it altogether as a historical source.
And in these circumstances the solution indi-
cated by Matthew Arnold seems to me the
best.   He considers, following more or less the
ancient tradition found in the Muratorian Canon,
that the work was issued in St. John's name,
and very likely with his approval, by one who
had gathered his materials from the lips of the
apostle.   Curiously enough this view has
received confirmation by the recovery of a
better text of another tradition about the
Gospel, parallel to that in the Muratorian
Canon.   The tradition I mean apparently goes
back to Papias, but it has hitherto been known
in so distorted a form that it has not attracted

the attention it deserves.   A late Greek *Catena Patrum* upon St. John contains the anonymous statement that John dictated the Gospel to his own disciple Papias.[1]   This is wholly improbable, and the case is not made very much better when we find the statement again in Latin, in a prologue to a Vulgate MS. of the Gospel, where we read that " the Gospel of John was manifested and given to the churches by John while yet in the body, as Papias . . . related : now he wrote down the Gospel, John dictating rightly."   At the same time so peculiar a statement, especially the phrase about John being yet in the body, could not be a mere invention as it stood.

But now we are in a position to carry back the story another stage.   In the magnificent edition of the Vulgate Gospels, lately published at Oxford under the auspices of the Bishop of Salisbury and Mr. H. J. White, you will find prefixed to St. John (p. 490) a very curious Prologue from the Codex Toletanus, a tenth-century MS. of the Vulgate, now at Madrid. This Prologue has nothing to do with the Vulgate.   It has evidently been translated from

---

[1] Corderius, end of Proem to *Catena in Joann.* : Ἰωάννης . . . ὑπηγόρευσε τὸ εὐαγγέλιον τῷ ἑαυτοῦ μαθητῇ Παπίᾳ.

the Greek, and its interest for us is that it contains the statements about Papias and the Fourth Gospel in a form which, if still not quite satisfactory, is at least much nearer the original than what we had hitherto possessed. It appears to me to be a transcript of the very account which St. Jerome used for his life of St. John in his *De Viris Illustribus*, that earliest " Dictionary of Christian Biography." After stating that John wrote last of all and at the request of the bishops of Asia Minor, that the Gospel was directed against Cerinthus and those who asserted that Christ did not exist before He was born of Mary, and that it relates the events of what happened in the two years before the Synoptic Gospels begin to tell their tale (all of which is to be found with verbal differences in St. Jerome), the Prologue goes on to say : " This Gospel therefore it is manifest was written after the Apocalypse, and was given to the churches in Asia by John while he was yet in the body, as one Papias by name, bishop of Hierapolis, a disciple of John and dear to him, in his *Exoterica, i.e.* in the end of the Five Books, related, he who wrote this Gospel at John's dictation (*Iohanne subdictante*). But

Marcion (*Archinon* Cod.) the heretic, when he was rejected by him because he thought the contrary,[1] was picked out by John. Now this person had brought some writings or letters to him, having been sent by brethren who were in Pontus, faithful in our Lord. Amen." [2]

Statements of this kind can never be altogether set aside until they are explained. Papias was certainly not the author of the Fourth Gospel, but the fact that his " five books " are mentioned is enough to show that we are not dealing with absolutely fabricated statements. It would be impossible to discuss this document at length in a lecture such as the present : I will therefore indicate what I believe to be the solution. Papias did not claim to report St. John, as we know from Eusebius, so much as the traditions preserved by the men of the next generation. His information about the Gospels was not first-hand, but from the " Elders " and other hearers of the apostles. I think some word has fallen out in the underlying Greek, and that the statement should run, not " as Papias related who wrote at John's

[1] *I.e.* Marcion thought the Gospels really were at variance.
[2] See Appendix.

dictation," but " as Papias related *from the man* who wrote at John's dictation." I should not wonder if in the original form of the statement " the disciple of John and dear to him " referred not to Papias, but to the writer of the Gospel.

Thus the tradition preserved in Codex Toletanus, and followed to so great an extent by St. Jerome, tells us in essentials much the same tale as that in the Muratorian Canon. The Fourth Gospel is written last ; it is written at the request of the Asiatic bishops ; and, most significant of all, St. John himself does not write, but a beloved disciple of St. John. St. John dictates, or rather suggests, for that is the meaning of ὑπαγορεύειν. This really satisfies most of the conditions of the problem : it is much easier to conceive the aged apostle approving the Gospel than actually planning and writing it down. But indeed the true value of the work consists not in the writer but in his materials. The Fourth Gospel enshrines many true words of the Lord which would otherwise have been lost to us. Like precious stones, their value does not depend upon their setting, and I confidently expect that many of them will come out safe from the laboratory of modern criticism, just as they have already passed safely through the apostle's memory and the evangelist's literary method.

(3) *The Gospel in Aramaic*

There is another side from which we can approach the sayings of Christ upon which I must touch, although it is more suited for a linguistic class than a popular lecture. The Gospels which we have are written in Greek, but our Lord and His disciples spoke in Aramaic, in the Semitic dialect current in Palestine at the beginning of our era. Thoroughly to understand our Lord's sayings we ought to be able to retranslate them into the original Aramaic.

Several efforts of varying merit have been made to do this, but none of them is satisfactory. The first and most serious difficulty is the individual style of the evangelists. They wrote in Greek and were less translators than adapters ; it is only here and there that we can be absolutely sure of the original wording. The Septuagint *is* a translation of the Old Testament into Greek, and we are often able by its aid to correct the transmitted Hebrew text, but we should not be able to reconstruct the original

Hebrew from the Greek alone. We must
therefore for the present abandon the attempt
to reconstruct St. Matthew's *Logia* in the
original Aramaic. What can be done, and
what has to a certain extent been done in
Professor Dalman's *Worte Jesu*—a book which
ought to be translated into English—is to
examine the leading ideas of the Gospels and
see what are their Aramaic equivalents. This
is not a task of merely antiquarian interest ; on
the contrary, it touches the very foundation
stones of Christianity. The world of Palestine
in which our Lord lived and taught, and whose
language He and His disciples spoke, is to us
nineteenth-century Europeans a very strange
far-off scene. The Gospels indeed are familiar
to us, but the background pre-supposed in the
Gospels is unfamiliar. The message of the
Gospel is in one sense universal, while human
passions and instincts remain what they are ; but,
in the first instance, it was a message adapted to
Palestine at a particular stage in the history of
the Jewish people, and if we are really to understand the message we ought to know the
thoughts of our Lord's first hearers and to be
acquainted with the religious phraseology in

which they clothed their ideas. If we are to
be impressed by the Gospel, we ought to be
thoroughly steeped in the questions which the
Gospel professed to answer. To do this one of
the surest ways is to collect, as Professor Dalman
has done, the current Jewish phrases found in
Targum and Talmud for the *Kingdom of God*,
for *Eternal life*, for the *Father in Heaven*, for
the pre-Christian conceptions of the Messiah
and the titles which the Messiah was to
bear.

By the aid of such investigations we can
learn which of two parallel phrases in our
Gospels more nearly represents the original, and
which is the later adaptation to Greek usage.
Thus, for instance, in such phrases as " Kingdom
of God " and the corresponding phrase " Kingdom of Heaven " characteristic of St. Matthew,
we learn that the genuinely Jewish phrase is
the Kingdom of Heaven (מלכות שמים). The
Jews avoided even the word *God*, as well as the
specially holy Tetragrammaton, and " Heaven "
was one of the standing substitutes for " God."
Moreover, the Kingdom of Heaven was not
used so much to denote the realm of the saints
whether in heaven or on earth, as to denote the

sovereignty of God : it means not the Church
but the Theocracy.

Still more important is it to learn what
besides the personality of Christ Himself, were
the really new and fresh elements in Christianity
I must not tresspass upon the province o
theology, so my illustration only touches doctrine
by a side issue. No utterance of our Lord is
more characteristic, if I may use the word, than
the prefixed *Amen* to solemn statements, which
our English versions render "Verily." Now it
is a remarkable fact that this form of associa
tion has no parallel at all in Jewish literature
They used "Amen" very much as we do, as
the answer to the leader in praise and prayer
or as solemnly affirming the words of another
Consequently therefore this "Amen," in such
phrases as "Amen, I say to you" was a
real peculiarity of our Lord's manner o
speech, and Dr. Dalman conjectures that it
was used by Him in logical agreement with
His own prohibition of all oaths. As St
Jerome puts it : "The *As I live, saith the Lord*
of the Old Testament is the *Amen, I say*
to you of the New Testament." [1] The evange

---

[1] Quoted by Dr. Swete on Mark ix 1.

lists seem to have been conscious that this
Amen was a real peculiarity, so they have left
it for the most part untranslated, an unassimi-
lated boulder out of the original preaching of
the Gospel.

In these two Lectures we have only been
able to touch the edge of a great subject : my
chief aim has been to show you the problems,
and the way that they are being attacked.   In
conclusion, I would say one word on the criteria
by which we have to test our working hypo-
theses ; in other words, how we are to find out
whether we are on the right track.   In historical
literary criticism, as in other departments of
human knowledge, Nature does not give us
theories, but only disjointed facts.   If we are to
understand the facts, we have to join them into
an organic unity by our theories.   If the
theory be false, the facts will refuse to fit in ;
but if the theory be true, other facts remote
from the subject in hand will be found to fit in
of themselves.   Or to put the matter in another
way, students who approach the subjects from
different sides will agree in their conclusions.
If our textual theories be right, the readings we

adopt will be approved by those who, like
Professor Dalman, work at the New Testament
from the side of Jewish Literature. If we are
going on the right track with regard to the
origin and composition of the Gospels, then
the next recovered document, whether it be a
papyrus from the dust-heap of an Egyptian
town or an overlooked fragment from a mon
astic library, will fall naturally into its place
strengthening our speculations and not upsetting
them. All this requires Time, which alone is
the infallible judge between the true and the
false, between that which is without foundation
and that which has been well builded.

NOTES

NOTE I

On the Story of the Woman taken in Adultery

THERE are one or two points connected with the recep
tion of the *Pericope de Adultera* in ancient times to
which I should like to draw attention, which involve too
much technical detail for convenient insertion in the
body of these Lectures.   Most of the textual facts are
given in Tischendorf *ad loc.* and in Westcott and Hort'
Note, but certain of the details call for some passing
remarks.

To avoid misconception it will be better to begin by
stating once more that it is absolutely certain that the
Story of the Woman taken in Adultery is no part of the
genuine text of the Gospel.   It interrupts the context, it
is written in a different style, and it is omitted by all the
oldest Greek and Syriac evidence.

The Greek Evidence

The *Pericope de Adultera*, by its mere length as well
as its intrinsic importance, stands out from most of the
passages disputed on textual grounds.   It was impossibl

for scribes not to be aware of its insertion or omission,
and accordingly we find that about one in five of the
MSS. which contain the *Pericope* contain also some
note to the effect that the passage is absent from many
copies. In some of these scholia the omission is justified
on the ground of its absence from the standard com-
mentaries of St. John Chrysostom, of St. Cyril of
Alexandria, and of Theodore of Mopsuestia ; it is also
stated that the *Pericope* is absent from the " more
careful " (*i.e.* revised) copies. All this expresses what
is obviously true : the *Pericope* was not accepted in the
revised versions of the fourth and fifth centuries either
in Antioch-Constantinople or in Egypt. It was at a
much later period that it found its way into the accepted
text of the Gospel, being read in many MSS. from the
end of the eighth century onwards. But so great an
innovation could not have been made for the first time
in the Byzantine age, and we actually find a series of
scholia asserting the presence of the section in " the
ancient copies " as follows :—

Λ (saec. ix) 262 (saec. x or xii) : τὰ ὠβελισμένα
    ἔν τισιν ἀντιγράφοις οὐ κεῖται, οὐδὲ ᾿Απολιναρίου·
    ἐν δὲ τοῖς ἀρχαίοις ὅλα κεῖται (followed by a refer-
    ence to the use of the passage in the *Apostolic
    Constitutions*).

135 (saec. x) 301 (saec. xi or xii) : εὕρηται καὶ ἔτερα
    ἐν ἀρχαίοις ἀντιγράφοις, ἅπερ συνείδομεν γράψαι
    πρὸς τῷ τέλει τοῦ αὐτοῦ εὐαγγελιστοῦ, ἅ ἐστι
    τάδε· (here follows the *Pericope*).

34 (saec. x or xi) : ἰστέον ὅτι διὰ τοῦτο μετὰ ἀστε-
    ρίσκων ἐτέθησαν τὰ περὶ τῆς μοιχαλίδος, ἐπειδὴ εἰς

τὰ πλείω τῶν ἀντιγράφων οὐκ ἔγκειται· πλὴν εἰ
τὰ ἀρχαιότερα ηὕρηνται.

It is the fashion to say that such scholia as these ar
" worthless." That is so far true in that they do ver
little to prove that the *Pericope* was the work of S⁺
John. But I see no reason for doubting the litera
truth of the statement that the section was contained i
some of the older MSS. known to the author or autho⁺
of the scholia. Moreover, notes of this kind were ofte
not composed by the scribe, but have themselves bee
copied from an older exemplar. Codex Λ is a MS. ⁺
the ninth century, but to judge from extant evidenc
very few MSS. from the fifth to the eighth centuries ca
have contained the *Pericope;* therefore the ancie⁺
copies referred to in Codex Λ probably belonged to
much older time, viz. the century of confusion betwee
Eusebius and St. Chrysostom.

But for one group which preferred the reading ⁺
the " old " MSS., half a dozen would prefer the readin
of the " correct " MSS. which were sanctioned by th
authority of the great Doctors. We therefore fin
distinct evidence not only for *non-interpolation*, but al⁺
for *excision.* Thus in the well-known minuscule 2
(= 565 Greg.) we read τὸ περὶ τῆς μοιχαλίδος κεφάλαι⁺
ἐν τῷ παρὰ Ἰωάννου εὐαγγελίῳ ὡς ἐν τοῖς νῦν ἀντιγράφο
μὴ κείμενον παρέλειψα· κατὰ τὸν τόπον δὲ κεῖται οὕτⁱ
ἑξῆς τοῦ οὐκ ἐγήγερται. In other words, the *Perico⁺*
stood in the usual place in the MS. from which 2ᵖᵉ w⁺
copied, but the scribe left it out intentionally for wh⁺
we may call critical reasons.

I have quoted these notes at length, because th⁺

illustrate the two points which must be kept in view :
(1) that the *Pericope de Adultera* was far too long and
far too striking to creep into a place in the text, so to
speak, unobserved ; and (2) that its rejection in the dominant texts of the fourth and fifth centuries actually led
later scribes and editors in some cases to leave the
section out, although it was contained in the exemplar
from which they were copying.

It is fairly obvious that the only sources from which
later Greek MSS. could copy the *Pericope* were other
MSS. of the Gospels.   One clear instance has been
pointed out by Mr. Kersopp Lake, who shows that the
text of the section in Codex 1071 (saec. xii) was copied
from Codex Bezae itself.   In such a case the *Pericope*
stands in its familiar though inappropriate position after
John vii 52, as in Codex Bezae itself.   But if a scribe,
who was copying from a MS. which contained the
section as a separate paragraph at the end of the
Gospel, desired to insert it in its place in the text, he
might very well insert it in the wrong place.   This has
actually happened in two cases :   Codex 225, a MS.
written at the end of the twelfth century, inserts the
section after John vii 36, and the " Ferrar MSS.," a
group of half a dozen closely-allied minuscules (all, except
one, of the twelfth century and connected with Calabria),
insert the section at the end of Luke xxi.   The Ferrar
group contains some other remarkable readings, and
had the text of the *Pericope de Adultera* which it
presents been conspicuously different from that of other
Greek MSS., we might have thought that this group of
MSS. had derived its text here by a peculiar channel

from the source whence the story was originally taken. But as a matter of fact the text of the *Pericope* as read by the Ferrar MSS. is neither striking nor peculiar, so that their eccentric insertion of it in St. Luke must have had its origin in some freak of editing, or (as has been plausibly conjectured) in some local peculiarity of Lectionary usage. It is inconceivable that the ultimate origin of the Ferrar text of the *Pericope* should be different from the ultimate origin of all the other Greek texts of the *Pericope*, *i.e.* a copy of the Four Gospels with the section inserted after John vii 52.

The Latin Evidence

The *Pericope de Adultera* is read after John vii 52 in the Latin Vulgate, in the Old Latin MSS. *e*, (*b**), *c ff*, and in the Graeco-Latin Codex Bezae (D*d*). It is quoted by St. Ambrose and St. Augustine, the latter of whom complains that some cut it out from their MSS. On the other hand, it is omitted in the Old Latin MS. *a*, in the revised texts *f*, *q*, and *l*, and in the ancestor of *r*. The page on which it was written in *b* has been cut out. It is not quoted by Tertullian or St. Cyprian.

The absence of early quotations is undoubtedly the weak point in the Latin evidence. That St. Cyprian should not quote the passage is not very surprising, as his only reference to the story of the woman in Luke vii 36-50 is a short and inaccurate quotation of the last clause of vii 47 (*Test.* iii 116). Tertullian's silence in *de Pudicitia* xi is more marked, but he himself supplies a conceivable reason why he and St. Cyprian after him should leave the passage alone. From their point of view the story *proves* nothing, it gives no basis for Church Law, because the woman was not a Christian. *Ad illa tempora quibus in terris egit hoc definimus nihil aduersum nos praeiudicare, si peccatoribus etiam Iudaeis uenia conferebatur. . . . Nemo Christianus ante Christum caelo resumptum* (Tert. *de Pudic.* xi).

That the story was unpopular in certain circles of the Latin Church is shown by its excision from *b* and the definite statements of St. Augustine (*Conj. adult.* ii 6). This would not be enough to exclude a genuine text from the canonical Scripture, but it might very well be enough to keep alive the knowledge that the passage was an interpolation, or in some way of inferior authority.

The text as actually transmitted in Latin falls into four families, viz. *e*, *d*, *c*, *ff*, and the Vulgate. These present much the same kind of in-and-out variation as in the rest of the Gospel. The most striking linguistic fact is the preservation of "i" (= πορεύου or ὕπαγε) in viii 11 by *e*. It is, I believe, the only instance of a monosyllabic derivative of *ire* in Biblical Latin. Its occurrence here at least suggests that the *Pericope* was not read aloud in the public services.

The Syriac and Armenian Evidence

Both in Syriac and in Armenian the *Pericope de Adultera* has found its way into the common printed editions, but in both cases we have clearly to do with a late addition of no critical value. Nevertheless, in each language more ancient forms of the story exist.

A copy of the Greek Gospels, which belonged to Mara of Amid during his exile at Alexandria (519-527 A.D.), contained the *Pericope*, either inserted after John viii 20, or more probably added at the end of the Gospel with a note that it belonged to Section 89.[1] From Mara's Codex it was cited in full by the Syriac translator and continuator of the *Ecclesiastical History* of Zacharias Rhetor, and from this source again it is quoted in Dionysius Barsalibi's *Gospel Commentary* at John viii 20. (See Gwynn, *Trans. of R. Irish Acad.* xxvii, pp. 291 ff.).

The text of the *Pericope* as printed in Armenian is an interpolation not much earlier than the ninth century, and most of the older MSS. omit it altogether. But in the *Expositor* for December 1895 Mr. F. C. Conybeare gives the translation of a very remarkable shorter recension of the story which he discovered in the same Edschmiadzin Codex of the Gospels that contains the note ascribing the longer conclusion of St. Mark to *Ariston*. This MS. is dated 989 A.D. Mr. Conybeare considers his shorter recension as the original form known to us. In his own words (p. 408) : "The shorter text of the Edschmiadzin Codex represents the form in which Papias and the Hebrew Gospel gave the episode. The longer form current is the same story edited, so to speak, for inclusion in the Greek Gospels at some very remote epoch."

I give below these two remarkable Eastern forms of the *Pericope :*—

[1] In error for 86. The Ammonian Section 89 begins at John viii 20 ; Section 86 contains John vii 26–viii 18.

Mara's Codex (as translated in the Syriac "Zacharias")

Edschmiadzin Codex of 989 A.D.

[Gwynn, *Tr. R. I. Acad.* xxvii, p. 292, note]

[Conybeare, *Expositor* for Dec. 1895, p. 406]

And it came to pass on a certain day, as Jesus was teaching, they brought unto him a certain woman which was found with child of adultery, and informed him concerning her. And Jesus said unto them (for he knew, as God, their lusts of uncleanness and their doings), "In the law what does it command?" Then said they unto him, "In the mouth of two or three witnesses she shall be stoned." But he answered and said unto them, "According to the law indeed one pure and free from these lusts of sin, and confidently and with authority (as being himself not guilty in this sin) bearing witness, let him bear witness against her and first cast a stone at her, and the next likewise, and let her be stoned." They then, because they were vile and guilty in this lust of transgression, went out one by one from before him and left the woman. And when they had gone forth, Jesus was gazing on the ground. And as he wrote in the dust thereof, he said unto her, "Woman, these which brought thee hither, and

A certain woman was taken in sins, against whom all bore witness that she was deserving of death. They brought her to Jesus (to see) what he would command, in order that they might malign him. Jesus made answer and said, "Come ye, who are without sin, cast stones and stone her to death." But he himself, bowing his head was writing with his finger on the earth, to declare their sins; and they were seeing their several sins on the stones. And filled with shame they departed, and no one remained, but only the woman. Saith Jesus, "Go in peace, and present the offering for sins, as in their law is written."

were desirous to bear witness against
thee, when they gave heed unto the
things which I said unto them,
which thou hast heard, have left
thee and departed : go thou also
now, and do not this sin any more."

Without necessarily endorsing Mr. Conybeare's view
of the Edschmiadzin text, we may acknowledge that it
has a decidedly ancient air, much more so than the
verbose paraphrase in the Syriac *Zacharias*. At the
same time it shares with it the omission of " Neither do
I condemn thee " in our Lord's speech to the woman, a
sentence which might seem too lenient for one who is
not stated to be even penitent. It is also somewhat
difficult to see why the Edschmiadzin Codex should
place the section after John vii 52, if it be a mere
quotation direct from Papias. The insertion of the
narrative at the same point that it is inserted in the
Western texts argues some community of origin, and
the absence of the *Pericope*, both from the *Diatessaron*
and all early forms of the Four Gospels in Syriac, makes
it improbable that it should have had a place in the
earliest form of the Armenian New Testament.

NOTE II

ON THE PROLOGUE TO ST. JOHN IN CODEX
TOLETANUS

CODEX TOLETANUS is an MS. of the tenth century,
containing the whole Bible in Latin according to the
version of St. Jerome, but with not a few traces of Old
Latin readings.   It is quoted by Wordsworth and White
as T.   Prefixed to St. John's Gospel is the ordinary
Prologue *Hic est Johannes*, etc., followed by a second
Prologue which is given below (*Wordsworth and White*,
p. 490).   I have inserted a punctuation and emended
the Spanish orthography of Codex Toletanus, but in all
cases of doubt the exact reading of the MS. is inserted
in the footnote.

Incipit Prologus Secundus

Iohannes apostolus, quem Dominus Iesus amauit
plurimum, nouissimus omnium scripsit hoc Euangelium,
postulantibus Asiae episcopis, adversus Cerinthum aliosque
haereticos et maxime tunc Ebionitarum[1] dogma consurgens, qui asserunt stultitiae suae prauitate—sic enim
Ebionitae[2] appellantur—Christum[3] antequam de Maria

---

[1] *ebonitarum* MS.   [2] *bonite* MS.   [3] *x͞p͞ni* MS. (?)

nasceretur non fuisse, nec natum ante saecula a Deo
Patre. Vnde etiam [4] conpulsus est diuinam eius a Patre
natiuitatem dicere.

Sed et aliam causam conscripti huius Euangelii ferunt [5] :
quia, cum legisset Matthei Marci et Lucae de Euangelio
uolumina, probauerit quidem textum historiae et uera eos
dixisse firmauerit, sed unius tantum anni in quo et passus est
post carcerem Iohannis historiam texuisse. Praetermisso
itaque anno cuius acta a tribus exposita fuerint, superioris
temporis antequam Iohannes clauderetur in carcere gesta
narrauit, sicut manifestum esse poterit his qui quattuor
Euangeliorum uolumine legerint diligenter.

Hoc igitur Euangelium post Apocalypsin scriptum
manifestum et datum est ecclesiis in Asia a Iohanne
adhuc in corpore constituto ; sicut Papias nomine Hieropolitanus episcopus discipulus Iohannis et carus in
Exotericis suis, id est in extremis quinque libris, retulit,
qui hoc Euangelium Iohanne subdictante conscripsit.

Verum Marcion [6] haereticus, cum ab eo fuerit reprobatus eo quod contraria sentisset, praelectus [7] est a
Iohanne : hic uero scripta [8] uel epistolas ad eum pertulerat [9] a fratribus missus qui in Ponto erant fideles in
Domino nostro. Amen.

The first part of this Prologue forms the beginning of
the article on St. John in the *De Viris Illustribus* of St.
Jerome : the last part occurs in a Vulgate MS. of St.

---

[4] *etqum* MS. (?)   [5] *fererunt* MS.   [6] *Verumarchinon* MS.
[7] *prelectus* MS.   [8] *scribtu* MS. (?)   [9] *pertulerut* MS. (?)

(Of these, Nos. 3, 4, 8 and 9 may be modern misreadings of
Visigothic script.)

John at the Vatican quoted by Thomasius. Both texts
are here given, the words which differ from the Prologue
in Codex Toletanus being in italics, and ∧ denoting an
omission.

De Viris Illustribus, c. IX.

Iohannes apostolus, quem ∧ Iesus ama*bat* plurimum, *filius
Zebedei et frater Iacobi apostoli quem Herodes post passionem
Domini decollauerat*, nouissimus omnium scripsit ∧ Euangelium,
rogatus ab Asiae episcopis, aduersus Cerinthum aliosque haereticos et maxime tunc Ebionitarum dogma consurgens, qui
adserunt ∧ ∧ Christum ante ∧ Maria*m* ∧ non fuisse ∧ ∧.
Vnde etiam conpulsus est *et* diuinam eius ∧ natiuitatem *e*dicere.

Sed et aliam causam *huius* script*urae* ferunt : qu*od*, cum
legisset Matthei, Marci Lucae ∧ uolumina, probauerit quidem
textum historiae ∧ uera eos dixisse firmauerit, sed unius tantum
anni in quo et passus est post carcerem Iohannis historiam
texuisse. Praetermisso itaque anno cuius acta a tribus exposita
fuer*a*nt, superioris temporis antequam Iohannes clauderetur in
carcere*m* gesta narrauit, sicut manifestum esse poterit his qui
diligentur quattuor Euangeliorum uolumin*a* legerint. *Quae res
et διαφωνίαν quae uidetur Iohannis esse cum ceteris tollit.*

Scripsit autem, etc.

I feel thoroughly convinced that St. Jerome has
borrowed from the document now represented to us by
the Prologue in Codex Toletanus, and not *vice versa.*
There are just the stylistic alterations that a rapid and
practised pen would make in borrowing a document for
incorporation in a Biographical Dictionary. The awkward
sentences in lines 5, 6 and 10 of the Prologue are curtailed,
while fresh though rather commonplace information is
inserted in convenient places such as the first sentence.

The parallel to the latter part of the Prologue runs as follows (*Thomasius*, vol. i., p. 344 = *Wordsworth and White*, p. 491).

Incipit Argumentum secundum Iohannem

Euangelium *Iohannis* ∧ manifesta*t*um et datum est ecclesiis ∧ ab Iohanne adhuc in corpore constituto ; sicut Papias nomine Hieropolitanus ∧ discipulus Iohannis ∧ carus, in Exotericis ∧ , id est in extremis quinque libris retulit ; *descripsit uero* Euangelium ∧ dictante Iohanne *recte*. Verum *Martion* haereticus cum ab eo fuisset reprobatus eo quod contraria senti*ebat, abi*ectus est a Iohanne. *Is* uero scripta uel epistolas ad eum pertulerat a fratribus ∧ qui in Ponto *fueru*nt ∧ . *Explicit Argumentum.*

Our Prologue, like most ancient fragments preserved as it were by accident, contains several obscurities. The parenthetical remark about the name of the Ebionites is probably a reference to the τῆς διανοίας πτωχεία which Eusebius and other Church writers profess to observe in them. The sentence about Marcion is very confused. I do not know what *prelectus* is meant for : Thomasius's text has *abiectus*, which might be held to imply *reiectus* in the common original, but the chronological difficulty still remains. The questions raised by the clause about Papias can scarcely be settled by emending the Latin, for the definite statement in Corderius that "John dictated the Gospel to his own disciple Papias" shows that a Greek tradition also existed to this effect. An adequate discussion of this tradition would involve an investigation into the various forms of the "Prochorus Legend," and a careful examination of the details of the evidence in the Muratorian Canon. My aim in writing this note has

been less ambitious, viz. to draw attention to the importance of the Prologue in Codex Toletanus, and to record
my conviction that it gives the earliest form known to us
of a very remarkable theory of the origin of the Fourth
Gospel.

That the rarer Prologues and Prefaces in Codex
Toletanus are derived from a very ancient source is
also suggested by the occurrence of *colobodactilus* in one
of them as an epithet of St. Mark (*Wordsworth and
White*, p. 171). This title for the evangelist is found in
Hippolytus (Μάρκος ὁ κολοβοδάκτυλος, *Haer.* vii 30),
but nowhere else.

THE END